Integrating Internal Displacement in Peace Processes and Agreements

Integrating
INTERNAL
DISPLACEMENT
in Peace Processes
and Agreements

Lead Author: Gerard Mc Hugh

United States Institute of Peace
Washington, D.C.

BROOKINGS

Ḃ   BROOKINGS-BERN PROJECT ON INTERNAL DISPLACEMENT

The Peacemaker's Toolkit Series Editors: A. Heather Coyne and Nigel Quinney

The views expressed in this report are those of the authors alone. They do not necessarily reflect views of the United States Institute of Peace.

United States Institute of Peace
1200 17th Street NW, Suite 200
Washington, DC 20036-3011

Phone: 202-457-1700
Fax: 202-429-6063
E-mail: usip_requests@usip.org
Web: www.usip.org

First published 2010.

Printed in the United States of America

The paper used in this publication meets the minimum requirements of American National Standards for Information Science—Permance of Paper for Printed Library Materials, ANSI Z39.48-1984.

Library of Congress Cataloging-in-Publication Data

McHugh, Gerard.
  Integrating internal displacement in peace processes and agreements / Gerard McHugh.
    p. cm. — (The peacemaker's toolkit series)
  Includes bibliographical references.
  ISBN 978-1-60127-051-1 (pbk. : alk. paper)
  1. Peace-building. 2. Peace-building—Social aspects. 3. Internally displaced persons.
  4. Refugees. 5. Migration, Internal. 6. Forced migration. I. Title.
  JZ5538.M3595 2010
  325'.21—dc22
                          2009039639

Contents

Foreword

One of the gravest humanitarian consequences of armed conflict is the displacement of populations. Those who are forced to flee and leave everything behind are often the victims who suffer the most. Their voices are seldom heard in peace negotiations, and yet realizing durable solutions for them is a crucial element for lasting peace. Return of internally displaced populations is often used as a benchmark against which progress in post-conflict stabilization and peacebuilding is measured. Durable solutions can best be achieved if issues related to internal displacement are addressed in peace agreements.

The report *Addressing Internal Displacement in Peace Processes, Peace Agreements, and Peace-Building* of the Brookings-Bern Project on Internal Displacement, which was released in September 2007, concluded that internal displacement has often been addressed in an ad hoc manner in peace processes and peace agreements. Drawing on case study analyses and consultations, the document echoed the recommendation of mediators, diplomats, UN representatives, and donors to develop guidance for mediators focusing specifically on incorporating internal displacement in peace initiatives.

This guide was developed in response to that recommendation. It gives practical guidance to mediators on how to integrate internal displacement in peace negotiations, how to incorporate issues pertaining to internal displacement into peace agreements, and how to engage the internally displaced persons themselves in the peace process.

Production of this guide was undertaken with guidance from a steering committee chaired by the representative of the UN secretary-general on the human rights of internally displaced persons and composed of senior mediators and leading experts on internal displacement, in close cooperation with the United Nations Mediation Support Unit within the

Department of Political Affairs, and in consultation with experts on mediation, peacemaking, and internal displacement. The lead author in drafting this guide was Gerard Mc Hugh.

Walter Kälin

Representative of the United Nations Secretary-General on the Human Rights of Internally Displaced Persons

Chris Coleman

Chief, United Nations Policy Planning and Mediation Support Unit, Department of Political Affairs, United Nations

Introduction

This guide provides mediators and their teams with practical guidance on integrating the human rights and interests of internally displaced persons (IDPs) into peace processes and peace agreements. Achieving such integration will not only safeguard the rights and interests of IDPs as stakeholders in a peace process but also assist mediators in fulfilling their core mission of helping the parties to the conflict reach a negotiated and sustainable settlement. By engaging IDPs in the peace process and integrating their interests in any agreed-upon settlement, mediators can create broader "buy in" and ownership of the process. By addressing durable solutions to internal displacement—i.e., return, local integration, or settlement in another part of the country—mediators can enhance the prospects of securing a viable agreement, sustaining its implementation, and building peace.

Although integrating internal displacement can be an essential component of a sustainable peace, it has often been addressed weakly or in an ad hoc manner during mediation efforts and in peace agreements. For instance, as shown in appendix 1 of this guide, out of nine recent peace agreements drawn up to resolve conflicts involving significant internal displacement, only three incorporated strong provisions on displacement. These examples and other past experiences highlight a need for guidance on how to better integrate internal displacement into peace processes.

Definition of Internally Displaced Persons

As defined in the introduction to the Guiding Principles on Internal Displacement (UN Doc. E/CN.4/1998/53/Add.2), internally displaced persons are "persons or groups of persons who have been forced or obligated to flee or to leave their homes or places of habitual residence, in particular as a result of or in order to avoid the effects of armed conflict, situations of generalized violence, violations of human rights, or natural or human-made disasters, and who have not crossed an internationally recognized State border."

This guide responds to that need. The framework and guidance presented here can directly assist mediators in their work in a number of ways, including by explaining how to

➤ create space within peace processes for consultation with, or even for the participation of, IDPs;

➤ identify those IDP-specific human rights and interests that should be reflected in peace agreements; and

➤ keep the end goal in view and avoid political manipulation of internal displacement.

Each of the following chapters focuses on one of four interconnected areas. These areas are termed "steps" because together they describe an overall process, but it is important to emphasize that the steps are not sequential so much as iterative, that all overlap, and some should be performed throughout the entire process.

➤ Step 1 addresses the question of "why": it presents the reasons for integrating internal displacement in peace processes and peace agreements.

➤ Step 2 deals with questions of "why" and "how": it discusses approaches to integrating internal displacement, including conceptual frameworks and legal and policy foundations.

➤ Step 3 focuses on "how" and "who": it looks at the process by which IDPs can be engaged in the various stages of a peace process.

➤ Step 4 explores the issue of "what": it offers guidance on the content of displacement-specific provisions that should be incorporated into a peace agreement.

As discussed in Step 3, when it comes to the process-related aspects of integrating internal displacement, IDPs can contribute to or participate in the peace process in a variety of ways; there is no one-size-fits-all solution. One of the objectives of this guide is to assist mediators in deciding on the most appropriate process for integrating internal displacement in a given context. In some cases, integrating internal displacement may be best accomplished through consultations undertaken separately from negotiations between the parties to the conflict. In other instances, consultations may be undertaken as part of the mediator-led process or in close connection with that process. Direct participation of IDPs at the negotiating table is also possible, although it has been the rare exception in past peace processes.

The level of detail to which the rights, interests, and needs of IDPs will be addressed in a given peace agreement depends on the context and the political dynamics of the situation. However, as discussed in Step 4, several key elements and topical areas should be considered in any agreement in order to find durable solutions to internal displacement.

It is important to note that IDPs do not lose any human rights entitlements and guarantees under international and national law that are available to the nondisplaced population in their country. They may claim additional protection and assistance to the extent that their displacement creates specific needs and vulnerabilities not shared by

IDPs and Refugees

In addition to displacing people internally, armed conflict often displaces persons to areas outside their country of residence, where they become refugees. The primary factual distinction between IDPs and refugees is that the latter have crossed an internationally recognized boundary and therefore are in need of international protection.[1]

The human rights and interests of all those who have been forced or obliged to flee—refugees and IDPs alike—should be integrated to the greatest extent possible in peace processes and peace agreements. Much of the guidance contained in this book concerning the process for engaging IDPs (Step 3) and the content of peace agreements (Step 4) is generally applicable to both IDPs and refugees. However, the primary focus is on internal displacement because of the particular consequences it can have for mediation efforts.

For instance, IDPs often remain in conflict zones and have needs and are afforded protections different from those of refugees (e.g., IDPs return or resettle earlier and more spontaneously than refugees and are more affected by issues of security during and immediately after the conflict). These specific needs must be addressed in peace processes and peace agreements.

Another way in which IDPs present a different challenge to mediators than do refugees is that whereas the latter are provided explicit protection under international law, IDPs do not enjoy explicit and specific legal protection. As a result, peace agreements that reflect the specific human rights and needs of IDPs can significantly enhance the protection afforded to IDPs.

nondisplaced people. This guide focuses on the human rights and specific protections under international humanitarian law that are *most* pertinent to IDPs because of their particular needs and circumstances.

The guidance presented here reflects and complements the principles contained in the Guiding Principles on Internal Displacement (described in more detail under Step 2 and summarized in appendix 2). This guide also builds on lessons learned from previous mediation initiatives and draws from past practice in drafting and implementing peace agreements. Appendix 3 directs the reader to additional information with a summary listing of useful resources. The Resource Kit that accompanies this guide contains a variety of reference materials, including the text of legal instruments.

Given that each conflict and peace process is unique, this guide is not intended as a rigid, one-size-fits-all approach for mediators. Nor does it delve deeply into approaches designed for different types of peace initiatives and different mediation "tracks" (Track I, Track II, Track III). Rather, the guidance is intended as a starting point from which mediators can tailor their own strategies to integrate internal displacement.

The Peacemaker's Toolkit

This handbook is part of the series *The Peacemaker's Toolkit,* which is being published by the United States Institute of Peace.

For twenty-five years, the United States Institute of Peace has supported the work of mediators through research, training programs, workshops, and publications designed to discover and disseminate the keys to effective mediation. The Institute—mandated by the U.S. Congress to help prevent, manage, and resolve international conflict through nonviolent means—has conceived of *The Peacemaker's Toolkit* as a way of combining its own accumulated expertise with that of other organizations active in the field of mediation. Most publications in the series are produced jointly by the Institute and a partner organization. All publications are carefully reviewed before publication by highly experienced mediators to ensure that the final product will be a useful and reliable resource for practitioners.

The Online Version

There is an online version of *The Peacemaker's Toolkit* that presents not only the text of this handbook but also connects readers to a vast web of information. Links in the online version give readers immediate access to a considerable variety of publications, news reports, directories, and other sources of data regarding ongoing mediation initiatives, case studies, theoretical frameworks, and education and training. These links enable the online *Toolkit* to serve as a "you are here" map to the larger literature on mediation.

Assess the Causes, Dynamics, and Characteristics of Internal Displacement

If they are to address internal displacement in peace processes adequately, mediators must be clear about the role of internal displacement. Why does internal displacement matter for peace? What are the characteristics and dynamics of internal displacement? What role can or should IDPs play in the peace process? This section provides guidance to assist mediators in addressing these questions.

Be Clear about Why Internal Displacement Matters for Peace

The guidance presented here is premised on the assertion—deduced from lessons learned from previous peace processes and consultations with IDPs—that in situations of conflict where persons have been forcibly displaced from their homes, the viability and sustainability of peace initiatives often will be linked with the participation of IDPs in the peace process and the integration of their human rights and interests in any agreed-upon outcomes.

In some situations, the main parties to a peace process may agree from the outset that internal displacement must be addressed because its relevance for peace is evident. Often, however, this is not the case, and mediators must in the first instance explain to or persuade the parties why internal displacement should be integrated into the peace process and any agreed-upon outcome.

The Scale of Displacement

As of December 2008, an estimated 26 million persons were displaced internally as a result of conflicts worldwide, more than one-and-a-half times the number of refugees.

Category of Forced Displacement	Total (millions)
Refugees under UNHCR mandate	10.5
Refugees under UNWRA mandate	4.7
Total number of refugees	15.2
Conflict-generated IDPs	26.0
Total number of refugees and conflict-generated IDPs	**41.2**

Source: Office of the United Nations High Commissioner for Refugees (UNHCR), 2008 Global Trends: Refugees, Asylum-seekers, Returnees, Internally Displaced and Stateless Persons (Geneva: UNHCR, June 2009), 3.

In making such arguments, mediators may want to draw from the following seven points, which highlight why internal displacement matters for peace:

> *IDPs can be important stakeholders in peace processes.* The fact that they have become displaced means that IDPs have already been significantly affected by the conflict and thus have much at stake in the outcome of the peace process. IDPs may be victims of the conflict, but they may also have been actively engaged in the conflict, which is another reason why they can be key stakeholders.

> *IDPs may directly affect the peace process in positive or negative ways.* Integrating internal displacement can enhance the breadth and depth of "buy in" for the process and any agreed-upon outcome. A wider sense of ownership will in turn strengthen peace initiatives and boost the prospects for their successful implementation. Moreover, IDPs may provide political support to or may be otherwise associated with parties to the conflict. They can influence, and can be influenced by, the parties to the conflict.

> *IDPs have specific needs that may remain neglected if the peace process and peace agreement do not specifically address them.* Like other persons, IDPs have rights and are afforded protections during and following armed conflict under international law. However, IDPs often have

specific needs and experience vulnerabilities that are different from those of nondisplaced groups affected by the conflict.

➤ *Addressing IDPs' needs and interests helps to address the causes of the conflict.* Addressing the needs and interests of IDPs—for example, by ensuring their ability to safely return home or resettle elsewhere—can assist in resolving some of the causes of the conflict. Conversely, the failure to address IDPs' needs and interests can cause tensions in fragile post-conflict settings.

➤ *Ending internal displacement is not possible without peace, and addressing internal displacement is essential to building peace.* Although it is true that IDPs are sometimes able to return to their homes before the end of hostilities, usually they cannot do so. As long as insecurity prevails or local communities are not ready to accept returnees, durable solutions to displacement will not be possible. Failure to address displacement can generate tensions between IDPs and host communities, provoke the rejection of any peace agreement by the displaced community, and nurture latent disputes and grievances that can constrain peacebuilding.

➤ *Internal displacement is often one of the most significant legacies of armed conflict, placing huge burdens on societies emerging from conflict.* Arrangements for addressing internal displacement in a way that lessens the burden imposed by displacement improve the prospects of peacebuilding.

➤ *Integrating internal displacement opens the door to future political participation.* Engaging IDPs in a peace process can prime them for more active participation in public affairs during the post-conflict transition. Furthermore, by facilitating participation of or consultation with IDPs during a peace process, the parties can demonstrate (to IDPs) their willingness to consider the needs and interests of displaced communities, and can therefore build or solidify potential future political constituencies. Especially in cases where IDPs are not identified with just one party to the conflict, this type of political argument may be persuasive in encouraging the parties to integrate internal displacement into the peace process.

For these reasons, mediators should seek to help the parties to the conflict and other stakeholders to develop workable, long-term solutions to internal displacement. Doing so can help break the cycle of conflict portrayed in figure 1. In this way, integrating internal displacement takes on an important preventive, as well as protective, role.

Possible solutions to internal displacement that allow displaced people to resume normal lives can be achieved through:

➤ return to and reintegration at the IDP's home or habitual place of residence,

➤ local integration in areas where internally displaced persons take refuge, or

➤ settlement in another part of the country.

For return, local integration, or settlement in another part of the country to be durable, such solutions must ensure long-term safety and security, equitably address property issues, and enable displaced persons to sustain their lives under normal conditions. Without these types of solutions, peace may be short-lived. Of course, no two situations of internal displacement are the same, so the role of IDPs and the prominence accorded to their interests will be specific to each context.

Figure 1. Breaking the Cycle of Displacement

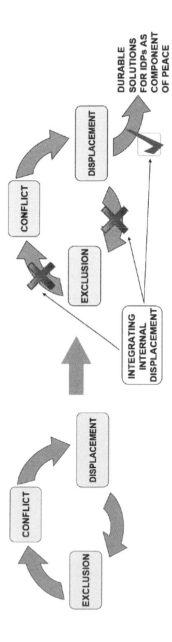

Understand the Causes and Patterns of Displacement and the Roles of the Parties

Understanding the causes of displacement and the roles of the parties in displacement can help mediators work toward solutions that address the particular situation of displacement as well as gain an understanding of the feasibility of other aspects of a peace agreement, such as disarmament, demobilization, and reintegration (DDR) arrangements and security measures to facilitate return or settlement elsewhere in the country. For instance, reintegration of former combatants is sure to fail if their communities are still in displacement when DDR programs are implemented.

Questions for the mediator to consider relating to the *causes* of displacement include the following:

➤ Did people flee in order to escape the general dangers of conflict or were they ordered to leave?

➤ Was the displacement part of a campaign to force a certain group from their home communities, i.e., an "ethnic cleansing" campaign?

➤ Who forced people to flee?

➤ Is the displacement asymmetric (only one party to the conflict is displacing civilians) or symmetric (parties to the conflict are displacing civilians thought to belong to other parties)?

Questions for the mediator to consider relating to the *patterns* of displacement include the following:

➤ Was the displacement spontaneous or organized?

➤ Was the displacement en masse at a specific time or in phases/waves?

➤ Where did IDPs go?

➤ Where are they now?

➤ Have any IDPs returned or decided to settle elsewhere?

Understand the Characteristics of IDP Groups

Among the various characteristics that IDP groups exhibit, a number are particularly important from the perspective of the mediator. Some are important because they highlight the nature of a group's relationships with the parties to the conflict, and thus help the mediator identify, for instance, the extent to which IDPs may be susceptible to the direct influence of the parties. Others are important because the nature and history of displacement, as well as the relationship of IDPs to nondisplaced populations, will influence the needs, interests, and priorities of IDPs. Table 1 spotlights several of these highly salient characteristics.

Table 1. Key Characteristics of IDP Groups

Characteristics of IDP Groups	Implications for the Mediator
May have political linkages to belligerents	IDP groups may provide political support to one or more parties to the conflict. IDPs may be in a position to exert influence over the parties, and conversely, political and/or military leaders within the parties may exert significant influence over IDPs. Mediators should examine the affiliations between IDPs and parties to the conflict and take into account to what extent these affiliations result in the political instrumentalization of IDPs.
Will have a displacement history	The length of time a group has been displaced, the number of times it has been displaced, and the type of displacement it has experienced form part of the group's displacement history. Mediators should learn as much as possible about this history of displacement, which will inform efforts to reach a peace settlement that includes durable solutions for internal displacement.
May spawn new/ competing leadership structures	IDP groups—having been displaced from their own communities and leadership structures and often scattered across a region or country—may well form new or competing leadership structures. Mediators should analyze to what extent these new or competing leadership structures may impact the peace process.

Will have a relationship with the host community	Mediators need to be cognizant of the relationship between IDPs and their host communities. The nature of such relationships can range from empathy to support and tolerance to hostility. Mediators should be careful that, by engaging the IDP community, they are not perceived as neglecting host community interests.
May stay within or outside camps	Mediators should ensure that they consult with IDPs living outside camps (e.g., in a host community) as well as those living in camps. Mediators tend to travel only to the most easily accessible camps to consult with IDPs, which can result in a distorted view of IDPs' needs and opinions.
Will have priority issues in mind specific to their situation	Like the parties to the conflict, IDPs will prioritize the issues that most acutely affect them. Mediators should try to ensure that these priorities are reflected in the peace process and the content of any peace agreement.

While all IDP groups will exhibit some of the same characteristics, mediators should avoid the trap of viewing IDPs as a monolithic bloc with homogeneous interests. Different IDP groups within a country will have different interests and loyalties. Even IDPs who come from the same communities may not share the same needs and views. Furthermore, the characteristics displayed by members of an IDP group in one part of the country may differ from the characteristics of members of the same group located in another part of the country. The interests of IDPs may mirror or deviate significantly from the interests within the nondisplaced population. Mediators should solicit the broadest possible range of IDP perspectives so as to avoid forming an inaccurate and oversimplified picture of the range of opinion within the IDP community as a whole.

Table 2 zeroes in on three factors that can significantly influence the participation of IDPs in the peace process: political support among IDP groups for belligerents, time spent displaced, and linkage between internal displacement and causes of the conflict. How each factor can affect the mediator's work is determined by the relative strength of the factor in a given situation.

Table 2. Implications for Mediators of the Strength of Three Key Factors

Weak/Low	Factor	Strong/High
➤ It may be easier to engage IDPs purely on the substantive issues affecting them, without those issues becoming politicized. ➤ The potential for IDPs to form political constituencies in the future can provide an incentive for the parties to address the interests of displaced persons early in the process.	Political support among IDP groups for belligerents	➤ Parties may be more responsive to the perspectives and interests of IDPs. ➤ IDPs may demand that their interests are more prominently reflected in issue areas that go beyond those specific to internal displacement (e.g., in power-sharing arrangements). ➤ IDPs may not express their true interests and may instead be used by the parties to convey the parties' messages.
➤ IDP groups may not have organized internally (e.g., within camps or host communities), and therefore mediators may have difficulty identifying interlocutors and soliciting perspectives. ➤ It may be difficult to engage on issues that are perceived as longer-term concerns. Mediators can begin consultations on issues relating to the immediate needs and interests of IDPs.	Duration of displacement	➤ IDP community may have organized internally, which may assist mediators in identifying bona fide community representatives. ➤ Leadership structures have had time to evolve to the stage that they may compete with traditional or home community leadership structures. ➤ IDPs may have developed clear interests and choices on return and settlement elsewhere in the country.
➤ Internal displacement may be used as an issue on which to gain consensus among the parties before moving to other, potentially more controversial issues.	Linkage between internal displacement and causes of conflict	➤ The implementation of provisions that address the causes of the conflict should include stronger roles for IDPs (e.g., IDP participation in land commissions).

Evaluate the Role of IDPs as Actors in the Peace Process

Having assessed the causes, characteristics, and patterns of displacement, the mediator will need to evaluate the potential role of IDPs as actors in a peace process based on

- the size of displaced group(s),

- the degree of leverage that IDPs can exert on the parties,

- security considerations associated with the involvement of IDPs and IDP representatives in a peace process, and

- the potential risk of IDPs acting as spoilers in the process.

Ultimately, the mediator will need to balance these considerations against the degree of ease or difficulty associated with extracting from the parties a commitment to integrating internal displacement during the process and in any resulting agreement. For example:

- If the parties are not strongly committed to the provisions of a proposed agreement relating to internal displacement, and if IDP groups have the potential to be spoilers (e.g., by rejecting other parts of the agreement, such as provisions on land use and elections), the mediator should try to involve IDP groups more actively and directly in the process. In such cases, the mediator should assess the most important issues of concern to IDP groups (i.e., the issues that may cause them to exercise their spoiling ability).

- If one or more parties are reluctant to make concessions and commitments to reach an agreement, and if IDP groups have strong influence over the parties, the mediator may wish to engage actively (and transparently) with IDP groups to highlight the role of the parties in delivering commitments and concessions such that internal displacement can be adequately reflected in any agreement. This understanding may encourage the IDP groups to exert influence on the relevant parties to reach agreement and/or make necessary commitments.

- In situations where IDPs may be perceived by one party to the conflict to support an opposing party, the engagement of IDPs in a peace process may pose unacceptable security risks for the IDP representatives. This danger is particularly acute in situations in which IDPs have been subjected to extensive or systematic violence during the conflict, especially when that violence is closely related to the cause of the conflict (e.g., ethnic cleansing). Parties may also have concerns that IDPs will identify perpetrators of the violence.

➤ If the IDP population is small in numbers and dispersed, if IDPs are unlikely to be able to spoil the process and any agreement, and if the parties are adamantly opposed to active IDP involvement or consultation, the mediator may need to make a pragmatic decision to engage the IDPs, if at all, remotely through intermediaries or partner organizations, rather than directly.

Create a Framework for Integrating Internal Displacement

This chapter presents a conceptual framework for integrating internal displacement in peace agreements and peace processes. It provides guidance on how the framework can be applied, in very practical ways, to assist mediators in their work.

This framework consists of three parts: a core mission statement for integrating internal displacement; legal and policy foundations, including the Guiding Principles on Internal Displacement and relevant provisions of international humanitarian and human rights law; and guidance on how to apply the mission statement and its legal and policy foundations.

In elaborating how the framework can be applied in a very practical way, Step 2 provides a lead-in to the discussions of process and content in Steps 3 and 4.

Use a Mission Statement to Guide the Overall Approach

The overall approach presented in this guide follows closely that used throughout the Guiding Principles on Internal Displacement (see appendix 2), which combines needs- and rights-based approaches. It views IDPs as a group with special needs within the broader population affected by conflict. In practical terms, this approach means the mediator will seek to ensure not only that those human rights and interests of IDPs that relate to their specific needs are incorporated in the peace process and peace agreement, but also that concrete, practical measures are taken to protect those rights and interests and address their needs.

Mission Statement: Integrating Internal Displacement

To facilitate the voluntary engagement of IDPs during the peace process and to ensure that the human rights, protections under international humanitarian law, and interests of IDPs are integrated in any peace agreement as a means of strengthening the process and enhancing the prospects for building peace, with a view to establishing conditions to end forced displacement by

➤ facilitating safe and voluntary return, local integration, or settlement in another part of the country;

➤ generating solutions to displacement that ensure long-term safety and security, that seek to equitably address property issues, and that ensure an environment that can sustain the normal lives of former IDPs in their settled locations; and

➤ preventing further forced displacement.

To assist in developing and implementing strategies for integrating internal displacement, mediators should develop a core statement of why they are working to engage IDPs in the peace process and to incorporate their rights and interests in any agreement. This kind of mission statement can assist the mediator in various ways; for example, it can explain to the parties the mediator's rationale for consulting with IDPs and it can provide the mediation team with a vision for integrating internal displacement. An example of this kind of mission statement is provided in the box above.

Understand the Legal and Policy Foundations

The foundations—in some cases, the mandate—for the integration of internal displacement in peace processes and peace agreements are provided in legal and policy instruments.

These foundations include the Guiding Principles on Internal Displacement, relevant national legislation, relevant provisions of international humanitarian and human rights law, and relevant resolutions and decisions of international organizations. Each of these components is described briefly below. The following sections provide guidance on how they can be applied in a way that helps the mediator integrate internal displacement.

Guiding Principles on Internal Displacement

Unlike refugees, IDPs are not protected by a specific international treaty, but as citizens or long-term residents of their country they fall under the protection of applicable international human rights and humanitarian law. The Guiding Principles on Internal Displacement codify and specify these human rights and specific protections relevant to IDPs under international humanitarian law by making explicit what is implicit in these more general provisions. They were developed in response to the need to ensure protection for IDPs and to provide a normative framework for that protection by compiling relevant international law concerning IDPs. The Guiding Principles were presented to the UN Commission on Human Rights in 1998 by the Representative of the UN Secretary-General on Internal Displacement.[7]

The Guiding Principles take the specific needs and vulnerabilities created by internal displacement as the point of departure and combine this "IDP needs-centered" approach to internal displacement with a "rights-based" approach identifying and setting out the rights and guarantees that meet those needs. The Guiding Principles—summarized in appendix 2 of this guide—are divided into five sections covering the various stages and conditions of displacement.

While the Guiding Principles do not constitute a legally binding text, they are based on and reflect provisions that are legally binding under separate instruments of international law.

The Guiding Principles have become an authoritative document setting out the principles for human rights and specific protections under international humanitarian law enjoyed by IDPs. As part of the outcome of the World Summit in 2005, the Guiding Principles were recognized by heads of state and government "as an important international framework for the protection" of IDPs.[3] The Guiding Principles have also been officially acknowledged by the African Union, its precursor the Organization of African Unity, and other regional organizations. The Organization of American States and the Council of Europe have urged their member states to incorporate the Guiding Principles into their respective national laws. For the states that have ratified the 2006 Protocol on the Protection and Assistance to Internally Displaced Persons to the Declaration on Peace, Security, Democracy and

Development in the Great Lakes Region, this incorporation into national laws is a legal obligation.The 2009 African Union Convention on the Protection and Assistance to Internally Displaced Persons in Africa builds on the Guiding Principles.

National Legislation

National authorities have the primary responsibility to provide protection and humanitarian assistance to IDPs within their territory and are bound to respect and ensure implementation of their obligations under international law to prevent internal displacement, protect and assist persons in displacement, and help them to find durable solutions. Some of these obligations are also relevant for de facto authorities, nonstate armed groups, and international actors.

The Guiding Principles are being incorporated into national legislation as well as IDP-related policies and strategies in a growing number of countries; many states have also ratified the international humanitarian and human rights law treaties that contain the rights and protections codified in the Guiding Principles. Therefore, domestic law of states experiencing internal displacement as a result of armed conflict may contain provisions that provide a foundation for integrating internal displacement. If so, national legislation can provide a useful entry point for the mediator in securing agreement from the parties on engaging IDPs in the peace process.

International Humanitarian and Human Rights Law

The provisions of international humanitarian and human rights law that relate to the rights and specific protections of displaced persons are reflected in and reinforce the Guiding Principles.

During armed conflict, the primary source of guarantees protecting IDPs is international humanitarian law, in particular the 1949 Geneva Convention relative to the Protection of Civilian Persons in Time of War (Fourth Geneva Convention), the two 1977 Protocols Additional to the Geneva Conventions, and the rules of customary international humanitarian law.[4] However, human rights law continues, in principle, to apply during armed conflict settings and becomes a main source of international law after the end of hostilities in post-conflict settings.

Figure 2. Relationship between Displacement-Specific and Displacement-Relevant Rights

Key: IHL—international humanitarian law
   IHRL   international human rights law
   GP—Guiding Principles

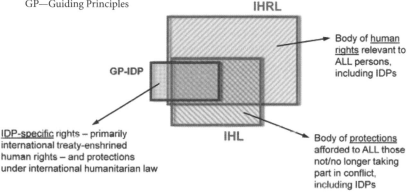

The Guiding Principles consist primarily (but not exclusively) of an IDP-specific subset of the human rights and specific protections under applicable international law afforded to persons in times of armed conflict. Thus, while all human rights will be relevant to IDPs ("displacement-relevant" human rights), certain rights ("displacement-specific" rights) may be particularly pertinent to IDPs because they address needs that the nondisplaced population does not have or that it experiences to a much lesser extent. The overlapping relationship between these different kinds of rights is shown in figure 2.

Displacement-specific rights include those relating to the prohibition of arbitrary displacement; the restitution of property and possessions left behind by IDPs during flight; protection against discrimination on account of being displaced; the replacement or reissuance of documentation left behind or lost during flight; the right to be protected against forcible return to danger zones; the right to vote even if due to the displacement it is not possible to cast the ballot at one's place of residence; and the right to decide whether to return, to integrate at the location to which IDPs were displaced, or to settle in another part of the country.

Some provisions of the Guiding Principles go beyond the explicit rights and protections in treaty-based international law but remain consistent with it—for example, the provisions of the Guiding Principles relating to rights and duties surrounding humanitarian access.

Mediators can use the Guiding Principles to identify and advocate for the rights of IDPs, but mediators may have to refer to specific provisions of international human rights and humanitarian law if the validity of any of the principles is contested by any of the parties to the negotiations. A set of annotations to the Guiding Principles has been drafted by Walter Kälin, the representative of the UN secretary-general on the human rights of internally displaced persons, to clarify and explain key aspects of each principle. This document is included in the appendices.[5]

International human rights law also contains important provisions relating to the rights of all persons to participate in political affairs, including peace processes. These provisions are particularly relevant to IDPs' participation in peace processes.

Resolutions, Declarations, and Decisions of International Organizations

Intergovernmental bodies and international organizations have made decisions through resolutions and statements relating to the human rights and interests of IDPs in peace processes and peace agreements. For instance, several Security Council resolutions have reaffirmed the right to return and the duties and obligations of various actors to facilitate the return of IDPs and refugees.[6] The UN General Assembly has also adopted resolutions regarding the rights and interests of IDPs. For example, Resolution 62/153 (2007) on the protection and assistance of IDPs (Paragraph 8), "Notes the importance of taking human rights and the specific protection and assistance needs of internally displaced persons into consideration, when appropriate, in peace processes, and emphasizes that durable solutions for internally displaced persons, including through voluntary return, sustainable reintegration and rehabilitation processes, and their active participation, as appropriate, in the peacebuilding process, are necessary elements of effective peacebuilding."

Regional organizations such as the African Union and the European Union have similarly contributed to the growing recognition of the status and protection of IDPs. Referring to IDPs, the Council of Europe emphasized that they "should be properly informed, but also consulted to the extent possible, in respect of any decision affecting their situation," prior to, during, and after displacement.[7]

Apply the Mission Statement and Its Legal and Policy Foundations to Assist Mediation Efforts

Integrating internal displacement in peace initiatives can bring with it significant challenges: the parties to the conflict may be reluctant to agree to IDP participation in the peace process; IDPs themselves may be reluctant to participate for a number of reasons; mediators may not have much to go on in regard to how displacement-specific human rights can be reflected in a peace agreement; time or logistical constraints may limit the mediator's ability to consult with IDPs; and so forth.

The mission statement and its legal and policy foundations presented above can assist mediators in overcoming some of these challenges, including by helping to

➤ create space for consultation with or even participation of IDPs in peace processes;

➤ identify those IDP-specific human rights and interests that should be reflected in peace agreements;

➤ keep the end goal in view;

➤ empower IDPs to contribute to peace processes; and

➤ avoid political manipulation of internal displacement.

The guidance presented here is specifically related to the application of the mission statement and its legal and policy foundations presented above and provides a point of entry for further guidance on process- and content-related dimensions of internal displacement presented in Steps 3 and 4.

Create Space for Consultation with or Even Participation of IDPs in Peace Processes

➤ If the parties to the conflict are reluctant to facilitate participation of IDPs in the peace process, the mediator can engage the parties with a view to highlighting the reasons why internal displacement matters (see

Step 1) and explaining the intended end goals (e.g., by referring to the mediator's mission statement for integrating internal displacement) and why the achievement of those goals is crucial for securing peace.

➤ To assist in this task of dialogue and (sometimes) persuasion intended to create a space for IDPs in the process, mediators can point to the Guiding Principles, international human rights law, and decisions of intergovernmental bodies to provide the rationale and justification for IDP participation. In particular, mediators may wish to highlight the following:

- Guiding Principle 22(d), which states, "[IDPs shall enjoy] the right . . . to participate in governmental and public affairs."

- Guiding Principle 28(2), which states, "Special efforts should be made to ensure the full participation of internally displaced persons in the planning and management of their return or resettlement and reintegration."

➤ The International Covenant on Civil and Political Rights (Article 25) and other human rights conventions referenced in the Resource Kit provide for the right of citizens to participate in public affairs, a right that arguably covers participation of IDPs in peace processes. When the parties are reluctant to facilitate IDP participation in a peace process, mediators can point to these provisions as providing a mandate for such participation.

➤ If any of the parties have backed themselves into a corner by initially pursuing a rejectionist line regarding the participation of IDPs from which it may be politically difficult to escape, the Guiding Principles and other foundations can provide a useful face-saving mechanism. The concerned parties can state, for example, that they are agreeing to IDP participation to assist in fulfilling the rights of IDPs.

Identify Those IDP-Specific Human Rights and Interests That Should Be Reflected in Peace Agreements

➤ In many cases of significant internal displacement associated with armed conflict, the human rights and interests of IDPs have been incorporated only weakly, or not at all, in peace agreements (see examples in appendix 2). The Guiding Principles and the human rights of IDPs under international law provide a framework guiding mediators

---

IDP Perspectives
Georgia: Ensuring IDPs Are Consulted in Decision Making

"The document on the integration of the IDP was not prepared with the participation of the IDP. That law was written for them without their involvement. When
the law on the IDP is written, their opinions should be taken into account. But
there, everything was done as the government wanted."

— *Mzia (53 years), IDP in Georgia (as captured by IDP Voices and available at http://
www.idpvoices.org.) IDP Voices is a collection of testimonies of IDPs published by the
Brookings-Bern Project on Internal Displacement.*

---

in identifying relevant needs of IDPs in a given situation (including ones
that may not be immediately obvious to all parties) and the
corresponding human rights that should be included in any agreement.

➤ Identification of the most pertinent human rights that are specific to the
situation of IDPs in any given context will be informed by assessing the
needs of IDPs and then relating IDPs' expressed needs to the relevant
rights. Mediators can gain insights on the needs of IDPs during direct
consultations, as well as indirectly from organizations or individuals
working closely with displaced communities. Relevant rights to address
typical needs of IDPs have been highlighted above and are further
elaborated upon in Step 4 below.

Keep the End Goal in View

➤ The mission statement provides mediators with an end goal to aim for,
while the legal and policy foundations provide the tools with which to
work toward that goal.

➤ The approach used in the Guiding Principles, which identifies pertinent
needs and the human rights guarantees that address these needs, can be
used by mediators as an example for how the entire peace process
should remain focused on the best interests of the people, even if not all
people are directly represented by the negotiating parties.

Empower IDPs to Contribute to Peace Processes

➤ Often, IDPs are not aware of their rights to participate in political
decision making, especially when those rights have been denied or have

not been exercised in the past. IDPs may be very eager to have their voices and perspectives heard but may not be aware of their rights to do so. Mediators—whether through direct consultations or through operational partners—can help to ensure that IDPs are aware of their relevant human rights and the protections they enjoy under international humanitarian law. Mediators can empower IDPs to contribute to, and even participate in, the peace process by engaging and consulting with them; working with other entities (e.g., UN agencies, local and international nongovernmental organizations) to provide as much information as possible on the process of consulting IDPs and other stakeholders; and highlighting the opportunities as well as the challenges of IDP participation.

Avoid Political Manipulation of Internal Displacement

➤ The issue of internal displacement can become politicized during negotiations between the parties, especially when the IDP community is politically homogeneous and/or when it strongly identifies with and supports one party to the conflict. The Guiding Principles and relevant provisions of international humanitarian and human rights law can be used as objective lenses through which to view internal displacement. That is, they can help the parties and the IDPs themselves see the substantive issues affecting IDPs rather than focus exclusively on political interests.

➤ By encouraging the parties to concentrate on the rights and protections of IDPs stipulated in the Guiding Principles and international humanitarian and human rights law, mediators will be better able to isolate the issue of internal displacement from potential political manipulation.

➤ The Guiding Principles can provide a point of reference for discussion of IDP rights and interests that will be politically neutral in any context.

Engage IDPs in the Peace Process

The participation of IDPs in peace processes is one facet of the broader effort of the mediator to reach out beyond the parties to the conflict and engage other constituencies, such as civil society organizations, traditional leaders, women's and youth groups, and religious groups.[8] The process of engaging IDPs, however, presents a distinctive set of considerations and challenges for the mediator. This chapter offers guidance on deciding how best to consult with IDPs and how to facilitate their participation throughout a peace process.

Assess Different Processes for Consulting with IDPs

According to the circumstances of a particular conflict, a range of options may be available to a mediator to integrate internal displacement into the peace process by engaging and consulting with IDPs. Three types of consultation processes are presented here; they have varying degrees of proximity to the mediator-led process:

➤ *stand-alone processes:* consultations on internal displacement (whether within the IDP community or between IDPs and parties to the conflict) that take place separately from the mediator-led process;

➤ *linked processes:* consultations on internal displacement that involve some degree of interaction with the wider peace process led by the mediator; and

➤ *inclusive processes:* consultations with IDPs that are undertaken as part of the process led by the mediator.

The relationships between these types of processes and the mediator-led process, and examples of each type, are presented in figure 3. That

Figure 3. Different Types of an IDP Consultation Process and the Mediator-Led Process across Four Stages of a Peace Process

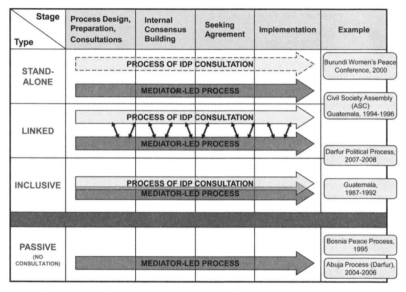

figure also shows a fourth type of process: the *passive process,* in which little or no consultation occurs with or within the IDP community.

These processes are not necessarily discrete. Some consultation processes, for example, may start off completely separate from the mediator-led process but may later be linked to the mediator's efforts to seek agreement between the parties or during the implementation stage.

Stand-Alone Processes

Stand-alone processes for consultation with the IDP community regarding a peace initiative take place separate from the mediator-led process. They may be initiated by civil society organizations, traditional or religious groups, or third-party facilitators as part of a Track-II peace initiative. This type of process often emerges when

➤ IDPs are organized into or affiliated with civil society organizations;

➤ the IDP community is frustrated with the pace or approach of Track-I initiatives;

- some or all of the parties are strongly opposed to the direct participation of IDPs in the peace process;

- third-party organizations are active in leading such a consultation process; and/or

- customary consultation processes are being actively used to facilitate dialogue among IDPs.

A mediator may have little or no influence over this type of consultation process (which is, by definition, separate from the mediator-led peace process) but should nonetheless endeavor to keep informed of its progress and identify potential opportunities to incorporate its results (e.g., insights into IDP perspectives) into the mediator-led process in the future.

Linked Processes

Linked processes for consultation with the IDP community exhibit cross-linkages and interaction between the IDP consultation process and the mediator-led process. Four models (Models A–D) of linked consultation processes, and their advantages and disadvantages, are presented in table 3.

Inclusive Processes

Inclusive processes are consultations with IDPs that are undertaken as part of the process led by the mediator. Two models (Models E and F) of inclusive processes, and their advantages and disadvantages, are presented in table 4.

Decide on the Type of Process

The most appropriate or most feasible process for consulting with IDPs will vary from one context to another depending on a host of local circumstances. Even so, mediators may wish to consider the following factors in making decisions on the type of process:

- *The parties' views of consultation with and participation of IDPs.* The views of the parties will strongly influence the type of process chosen for IDP consultation and participation. One or more of the parties may reject or be reluctant to agree to IDP consultation or participation directly in the negotiations (Model F), especially if IDPs support particular parties to the conflict.

➤ *The willingness and capacity of the IDP community.* IDPs may be reluctant to participate directly in the process or even to be present at the venue of any multilateral talks, particularly if IDPs have been targeted by one or more of the parties to the conflict. In such cases, stand-alone models or Models A or B may be most appropriate. In all cases, the mediator should ensure that the capacity of IDPs to participate matches the model for participation.

➤ *Nature of displacement: dispersed or collective.* The location and concentration of IDPs should influence the mediator's choice of consultation process. A more geographically dispersed IDP community, especially in insecure environments, can limit the ability of the mediator or intermediaries to consult actively with a representative cross-section of IDPs. Moreover, IDPs may be unable or unwilling to travel to a location distant from their settlement because of logistical shortfalls or security concerns. For these reasons, Model B or Model E may be the most appropriate form of consultation for a widely dispersed IDP community, while Models A or D may be more effective for an IDP community that is concentrated in a single area, assuming in both cases that the parties agree.

➤ *The mediation team's capacity.* Pressures of time and resources may make it difficult for the mediation team to undertake as broad a consultation process as it would like. In such instances, the mediator should consider adopting Model B or Model E.

Table 3. Linked Processes for Engaging IDPs in the Peace Process

Model	Description	Pros and Cons	What It Looks Like
A	Multilateral (mediation) with the parties; IDP remote participation linked through mediator	May be best suited to situations where IDPs are reluctant to directly engage with parties and where they view the mediator as an effective and reliable conduit for integrating their perspectives into the process. **Pros:** Provides mediator with direct contact with larger number of IDPs; may be easier to negotiate this form of participation with parties. **Cons:** Requires extensive travel and consultations (by mediator) in the areas of displaced persons during various stages (especially the "seeking agreement" phase); does not provide IDPs with direct exposure to parties.	
B	Multilateral with the parties; IDP remote participation linked through intermediary and mediator	May be useful if other entities (e.g., local or national nongovernmental organizations) have existing relationships with IDPs; the intermediary may have resources and contacts to facilitate consultations and forums in areas where IDPs are located. **Pros:** Reduces logistical burden on mediation team; leverages existing contacts and relationships. **Cons:** Introduces another entity into the chain of consultation between mediator and IDPs (i.e., a less direct mode of participation); does not provide IDPs with direct exposure to parties.	
C	Multilateral with the parties; IDP remote participation linked via party/parties	Can be an option if strong political support exists within group(s) of IDPs for one or more parties to the conflict and where these IDP groups agree to have their views and interests represented by the party. **Pros:** Advantage for IDPs is that they will have their interests injected into the process by a party of their choosing. **Cons:** More of a possibility that human rights and interests of IDPs will be discussed in the context of other political objectives. *Note: In this situation, the mediator should make sure that all the human rights and interests of IDPs are integrated into the peace process, not just those presented by a party.*	

Table 3. Linked Processes for Engaging IDPs in the Peace Process (continued)

Model	Description	Pros and Cons	What It Looks Like
D	Shuttle mediation with the parties and IDPs	When multilateral talks are not possible or desirable, mediator can shuttle between parties to mediate and shuttle between IDP groups to consult. **Pros:** Gets around parties' resistance to direct participation of IDPs; allows IDPs to contribute freely without fear of reprisals by parties. **Cons:** Does not provide IDPs with direct exposure to parties.	

Key: MED denotes mediator.
A, B, C represent parties to the conflict.

Table 4. Inclusive Models for Engaging IDPs in the Peace Process

Model	Description	Pros and Cons	What It Looks Like
E	Multilateral with parties; IDP representatives participate locally (at venue of mediated talks) through mediator	May be most appropriate in situations where IDP groups are highly organized and can select representatives to attend peace talks. **Pros:** Provides an opportunity for IDP representatives to directly communicate IDP interests to parties (at the venue of the peace talks); provides visible demonstration of commitment (by parties, mediator) to integrate internal displacement in the process. **Cons:** Mediators need to confirm IDP endorsement of the IDP representatives who attend peace talks.	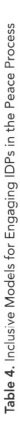
F	Multilateral with parties; direct IDP participation	**Pros:** Provides direct voice for IDP interests and human rights within the negotiations. **Cons:** Potentially exposes IDP participants to pressures from parties.	

Follow General Guidelines for Engaging with IDPs

Irrespective of the model of consultation they adopt, mediators using linked and inclusive processes for engaging IDPs should follow some general guidelines.

Seek Informed Consent and Be Clear about Expectations

➤ Secure the informed consent of IDPs to create space for their contribution to or participation in the process. Do not take for granted that they wish to participate in the peace process.

➤ Secure the informed consent of parties to the conflict to facilitate the participation of IDPs or IDP representatives in the process. Act in a transparent manner with the parties with regard to the need to ensure participation of IDPs in the peace process; discuss with them the expected role of IDPs in the process.

➤ Be transparent with IDPs with regard to the mediator's neutral interactions with the parties. Explain clearly the purposes and intended outcomes of their participation in the various stages of the peace process.

➤ Ensure that IDPs have realistic expectations regarding the time frame for the various stages of the process.

Be Available for Consultation and Communication

➤ Conduct consultations in a language that IDPs understand. Undertake consultations at a time and a place appropriate for IDPs to ensure their participation; be sensitive to cultural or religious observation times and customs when scheduling meetings.

Demonstrate Commitment to the Concerns and Interests of IDPs

➤ Whenever possible and appropriate, act decisively regarding the concerns and interests of IDPs and provide feedback to IDPs on challenges and opportunities associated with their participation in the peace process.

Design the Method of Consultation to Fit the Purpose

➤ Use methods of consultation that best fit the purpose and the model of representation. For example, larger meetings with a wider group of IDPs present an opportunity for providing information to a larger IDP audience. Smaller meetings may be more appropriate at later stages of the peace process to consult on technical issues (e.g., modes of return or settlement).

➤ Whatever the size of the meeting, solicit a broad cross-section of perspectives. IDPs may be reluctant to share contrary views in a large meeting. Therefore, hold several smaller meetings within a single IDP community.

➤ Avoid the pitfall of holding consultations with IDPs only in those areas that are easily accessible (e.g., in and around urban centers).

➤ Ensure an appropriate gender balance on the mediator's consultation team, bearing in mind that female team members may more effectively elicit perspectives from female IDPs.

➤ Ensure that that the interests and perspectives of children are reflected or presented in the consultations (e.g., solicit the input of youth groups). Especially in the case of lengthy displacements, children will have spent a significant proportion of their lives displaced and will have special needs (e.g., access to education).

Identify Representative and Credible IDP Interlocutors

➤ Consider carefully how to determine who represents or should represent IDPs in consultations and the broader peace process. Questions that can assist mediators in this regard include

- Are there leaders within the IDP community who are widely recognized within a particular IDP group (for example, a particular camp)? How were these leaders selected? What is their relationship with extant community leadership structures in the IDPs' home communities?

- Are existing IDP leaders representative of the ethnic, political, geographic, or tribal makeup of that particular IDP group?

- Within a group of IDP interlocutors or representatives, is there a

Ensuring the Participation of Women in Consultations with IDP Communities

In 2005, the United Nations Development Fund for Women (UNIFEM) published guidance for international actors on securing the effective participation of women—including displaced women—in all stages of peace processes.

UNIFEM's guidance asserts that the identification, early in the peace process, of strategic entry points for women's participation can significantly heighten their access to the bargaining table and their impact on any agreement. Recommended actions include

➤ Create a directory of women's civil society organizations through field-based consultations with women's groups and leaders, including internally displaced populations.

➤ Advocate with the negotiating parties and with IDP representatives for a minimum of 30 percent women's representation in their delegations.

➤ Work to facilitate meetings between women's groups, including displaced women (as part of broader civil society constituencies) and negotiating parties at various stages of the peace process.

➤ Support the establishment of a women's advisory committee to the negotiations process to include displaced women to track and advise the formal peace process.

➤ Ensure that consultative processes with displaced women feed directly into negotiations.

Source: United Nations Development Fund for Women (UNIFEM), *Securing the Peace: Guiding the International Community towards Women's Effective Participation throughout Peace Processes* (New York: UNIFEM, October 2005).

balance in terms of gender, age, and religion? Are there representatives (formal or informal) of women's or youth groups?

- Are there competing leadership structures within certain IDP groups?

➤ Encourage or insist upon the participation of female IDP representatives in any consultations with IDP communities.[9]

➤ Strive to engage with recognized traditional and tribal leaders who may be displaced, while avoiding the potential for exacerbating possible competing leadership structures that may be present or evolving within the IDP communities.

Ensure the Security and Confidentiality of IDP Interlocutors

➤ Assess possible security threats to IDPs, and use the results to conduct consultations and meetings in a way that does not expose interlocutors to risks (e.g., hold meetings with IDPs in venues other than IDP camps).

Engage IDPs throughout the Stages of a Peace Process

Mediators should seek to engage IDPs early in a peace process and to keep them engaged throughout its course. This section provides practical guidance on how to accomplish this. It divides the peace process into four stages: mediation process design, prenegotiation preparation, and consultation; internal consensus building; seeking agreement between the parties; and implementation. The guidance presented here relates primarily to the linked and inclusive processes for integrating internal displacement, because these are the two processes that will see the most interaction between the mediator and IDPs.

Stage I: Mediation Process Design, Prenegotiation Preparation, and Consultation

➤ Gather as much information as possible on the IDP community (taking note of the characteristics listed in table 1 above). Assess the level of coherence and political homogeneity within the IDP community.

➤ Identify linkages between IDPs and the parties to the conflict and the extent of support among IDPs for the parties.

➤ Drawing on existing studies and data, make a preliminary assessment of the interests of IDPs (e.g., as expressed to other interlocutors).

➤ Identify interlocutors within the IDP community and within host communities. Make initial contact with IDP representatives, either directly or through intermediaries.

➤ Engage in initial dialogue with the IDP community to explain the mediation mandate and the mediator's strategy and rationale for engaging IDPs in the peace process.

➤ Solicit the current interests and perspectives of the IDP community (recognizing that these interest and perceptions may change as the peace process evolves).

➤ Assess the capacity of the IDP community to participate effectively in the peace process.

➤ Engage with host communities to explain the reasons and modalities for IDP participation in consultations and to ensure that they do not perceive that their interests are being overshadowed by those of IDPs.

IDP Perspectives
Northern Uganda: Failing to Consult with IDPs

As of June 2007, knowledge among IDPs in Northern Uganda of what was happening at the peace talks between the Government of Uganda and the Lord's Resistance Army (LRA), ongoing since July 2006, was assessed to be "uniformly poor."

In a research study, only 4 percent of those surveyed said that they were well informed about the peace process. Many IDPs were not aware of the composition of the delegations to the peace talks and many also were unsure as to whether an IDP representative was present at the peace talks. "If I had a representative at the peace talks, that person would have come back during the recess and explained to us what had happened there," commented one of the IDP camp leaders. "And he would have also listened to our views in preparation for the next session."

In the words of a man from Mucwini camp: "The talks would be relevant to us if occasionally one or two representatives of the Acholi people now in Juba would come here and discuss the results with us and get our thoughts, but no one comes. Everything is hearsay."

Source: United Nations Integrated Regional Information Network (IRIN), UGANDA: Population out of Step with Peace Talks (Kampala: IRIN, September 24, 2007); Oxfam International, The Building Blocks of Sustainable Peace: The Views of Internally Displaced People in Northern Uganda, Oxfam Briefing Paper no. 106 (Oxford: Oxfam International, 2007).

Stage II: Internal Consensus Building

➤ Work with the parties to the conflict to create political space for the participation of IDPs (as described above in the section "Create Space for Consultation with or Even Participation of IDPs in Peace Processes").

➤ Provide or request others to provide capacity-building assistance (e.g., technical expertise) to IDP groups, as well as to the parties. Such capacity-building efforts should not privilege any group and should aim to provide a common basis for consultation and negotiations.

➤ Request that IDP groups consult internally to gain consensus (not consensus within the entire IDP community, but consensus within different IDP groups) on their key interests.

➤ Engage IDP interlocutors in a dialogue on practical modalities for their participation in the peace process, including in this internal consensus-building stage and subsequent stages. Practical arrangements to be discussed can include IDPs' identification of representatives/spokespersons, logistical arrangements, mechanisms to facilitate feedback of information from the process to IDP communities, and security considerations.

➤ Work with IDPs (whether directly or through operational partners) to develop and refine the practical modalities for IDP participation in the process emerging from dialogue among IDPs (see above).

Stage III: Seeking Agreement between the Parties

During this third stage, the mediator may pursue a number of approaches, including multilateral talks with the parties and/or shuttle mediation.

➤ Assuming that IDPs are not directly represented at the negotiating table, structure their participation so as to help the parties identify options. For example, when discussing the return and settlement of IDPs, the parties could benefit from hearing IDP perspectives on the nature and sequence of actions the parties will have to undertake to facilitate return or settlement elsewhere in the country.

➤ In situations in which parties have very different views on an issue that has implications for IDPs, use the perspectives of IDPs as a neutral (i.e., de-linked from the parties) basis for bridging the gap between the parties. This approach is most feasible in cases in which the IDPs are not closely aligned with any one group.

➤ If pursuing a linked approach, ensure active back-and-forth communication between the mediation team and IDPs or their representatives, especially on issues that relate specifically to IDPs.

➤ If an inclusive approach is being used, ensure that IDP representatives are feeding back information on the process and options being discussed (respecting the confidentiality requirements of the process) to the broader IDP population.

Stage IV: Implementation

Mediators may no longer be directly involved in a peace process during the stage at which an agreement is being implemented, but that stage will proceed more smoothly if the mediators have earlier put in place follow-up mechanisms (such as monitoring teams) to facilitate the process of implementation.

For the process-related aspects of implementation (content-related aspects are discussed in Step 4), mediators should do the following:

➤ Consult with IDP representatives or communities to solicit input on the desirability of IDPs playing a direct role in the implementation of any agreement and their capacity to do so.

➤ Work with IDP groups—through meetings and consultative forums—to identify areas in which they may need support in the implementation phase (such as external expertise) and to help provide that support.

➤ Ensure that the roles and responsibilities of IDPs during implementation are discussed with the parties and are clearly communicated to broader IDP constituencies.

Troubleshooting: How to Overcome Obstacles to the Engagement of IDPs

What can mediators do when confronted with significant obstacles or outright opposition to the participation of IDPs in a peace process?

In addition to the guidance offered in Step 2, the following recommendations may be of use to mediators in overcoming obstacles to IDP participation. Mediators should bear in mind, however, that in many instances integration of internal displacement may require significant compromises by the parties and indeed by the mediation team.

IDPs Have Disparate Views

In cases where groups of IDPs disagree on interests and priorities, the mediator or an operational partner may need to moderate between the groups to try to encourage a convergence of views so that the IDPs will have a more unified and thus stronger voice in the peace process. Where consensus cannot be achieved, the mediator should attempt to reflect the IDPs' conflicting or divergent views in the peace process. The mediator can suggest different models (including some of the options in table 3 and table 4) for the participation of different IDP groups. For example, some groups may opt to have their interests represented by one of the parties, while another group may wish to have representatives present at the venue of the talks.

The Parties Refuse IDP Participation

Faced with parties opposed to the participation of IDPs in the peace process, a mediator should first follow the advice provided in Step 2 and try to use the framework for integrating internal displacement to create space for IDP participation. If the parties continue to refuse IDP participation, the mediator may wish to consider the following options:

➤ Advocate with other stakeholders (e.g., the parties' international regional supporters) for IDP participation.

➤ Consider establishing a consultation mechanism that will feed IDP perspectives into the peace process through the mediation (akin to Model A or B in table 3)

➤ Invite the parties to suggest ways in which IDP perspectives could be integrated via civil society organizations.

➤ Suggest to the parties that IDPs provide inputs on specific technical issues (e.g., return or settlement elsewhere in the country).

➤ Make IDP participation a condition of the mediation.

Inadequate Resources or Time for Full Consultation

In situations in which the mediation team has insufficient resources or time to fully consult with IDPs, the team should treat every visit to an area containing IDPs as an opportunity to consult, formally or informally, with IDPs. The team should also seek to augment its knowledge of the interests and perspectives of IDPs by drawing on the experience of other actors who interact frequently with IDPs. Public information and outreach mechanisms (such as interviews on local radio stations) offer a way for the team to keep IDPs informed about progress in the peace process.

Integrate Human Rights and Interests of IDPs in the Peace Agreement

Every peace agreement is unique, of course, being tailored to the circumstances of the conflict it is designed to terminate. Thus, the guidance offered in this chapter on integrating the rights and interests of IDPs in a peace agreement should be regarded purely as a starting point from which a mediator can begin to shape the relevant sections of an agreement that fits the specific context of the conflict with which he or she is dealing. Examples of how the human rights and interests of IDPs have been incorporated into peace agreements are included throughout this section.

Consider Two Key Issues

In deciding what overall approach to take toward integrating internal displacement in a peace agreement, mediators should consider two key issues: whether to address internal displacement within the main body of the agreement or in a protocol, and whether to adopt a maximalist or pragmatic attitude toward IDP rights.

Where to Place Provisions on Internal Displacement

A peace agreement may include a small number of substantive provisions relating to internal displacement in the main text of the agreement, or it may include a more expansive range of provisions in an associated protocol (e.g., Annex VII to the Dayton Agreement). A third option is to create a follow-up mechanism (e.g., a mechanism to incorporate IDP issues into a wider peacebuilding strategy). These options are not mutually exclusive, and some combination of two or all three options is common. Mediators may therefore have to decide what provisions to include in the main text and what provisions to append by means of an additional protocol or follow-up process. Provisions relating to the most fundamental rights, protections, and interests of IDPs should be incorporated (even in summary form) in the main text, as should the main elements of implementation of IDP-specific provisions.

An example for the combination of the three options is provided by the Declaration on Peace, Security, Democracy and Development in the Great Lakes Region. The declaration, which sets out the framework for achieving peace and stability in the Great Lakes region, contains one article on internal displacement, referring to the Protocol on the Protection and Assistance to Internally Displaced Persons, while the protocol obliges states' parties to enact specific legislation in accordance with certain standards.

How to Balance Maximalist and Pragmatic Approaches

Ideally, all human rights and interests of IDPs will be adequately reflected in a peace agreement. In each situation, however, certain rights or interests will be most pertinent for that particular case, and it is these rights and interests that mediators should work to include as priorities. Such a needs-based approach to determining priorities requires a careful assessment of the situation on the basis of consultations with IDPs.

For example, in situations where one of the causes of the conflict and of displacement relates to disputed land ownership, consideration of and agreement on issues relating to the right of IDPs to choose return or settlement elsewhere in the country will likely be feasible only if the rights of IDPs and others to property ownership are considered and reflected in mechanisms for resolving land use or ownership disputes. The maximalist approach may auger for equal prominence accorded to *all* human rights and interests, and may in certain cases be possible, but in this example, where rights and interests relating to land ownership and/or tenure relate directly and intensely to the causes of the conflict, the mediator will need to place a high priority on integrating these most pertinent rights and interests, as well as the right to return home or settle elsewhere in the country.

The sequencing of implementation of provisions relating to priority rights and interests must also be considered when drafting the agreement; displaced persons will likely not be able to return home or settle elsewhere in the country until at least some of the security arrangements have been implemented and mechanisms have been identified for addressing land ownership or land tenure disputes.

Another situation in which the mediator may need to balance maximalist and pragmatic approaches is one in which one or more parties to the conflict strenuously object to the explicit inclusion of certain rights and interests of IDPs in a peace agreement. In cases where the mediator believes that the success or failure of the entire process may hinge on such a position adopted by one or more of the parties, a pragmatic approach may necessitate seeking inclusion, to the extent possible, of the highest priority rights and interests of IDPs, with other rights and interests of IDPs to be considered at a later stage. In such situations, the mediator can propose options to facilitate more complete consideration and fulfillment of the human rights and interests of IDPs at a later stage, such as through the establishment of a Commission on Internal Displacement.[10]

Focus on Four Areas

The findings of previous studies and lessons learned from past practice suggest that mediators should focus on four areas when seeking to incorporate the human rights and interests of IDPs in peace agreements:[11]

➤ incorporation of clear and consistent definitions pertaining to internal displacement;

➤ clear stipulation of displacement-specific human rights and specific protections under international humanitarian law reflecting the interests of IDPs;

➤ specification of roles and obligations of parties to the conflict vis-à-vis internal displacement; and

➤ specification of a clear implementation process, including the roles of IDPs.

Table 6. Examples of Use of Clear Definitions

Context	Draft/Final Peace Agreement	Provision	Comment
Uganda	Draft Agreement on Comprehensive Solutions between the Government of Uganda and LRA/M	"'Internally displaced persons' (IDPs) are persons or groups of persons who have been forced or obliged to flee or leave their homes or places of habitual residence, in particular as a result of or in order to avoid the effects of armed conflict, situations of generalized violence, violations of human rights or natural or human-made disasters, and who have not crossed an internationally recognized state border."	Provides the complete definition of IDPs from the Guiding Principles (quoted above in the Introduction) in the "Definitions" section of the agreement
Burundi	Arusha Peace and Reconciliation Agreement (2000)	"The term 'sinistrés' designates all displaced, regrouped and dispersed persons and returnees."	Clarifies the definition and use of the local term "sinistré"

Use Clear and Consistent Definitions

The use of clear and internationally recognized definitions for IDPs and refugees in peace agreements can help avoid confusion and ambiguity as regards to whom these provisions apply (table 6).

Options and guidance for mediators

➤ Include the definition of IDPs from the Guiding Principles (quoted above in the Introduction) in the peace agreement and be careful to avoid notions that exclude some IDPs (e.g., those displaced by government forces). Draw a clear distinction between IDPs and refugees. Use the definition of "refugee" from the Convention relating to the Status of Refugees (1951) and the Protocol relating to the Status of Refugees (1967), or the wider notions of "refugee" as embodied in applicable regional instruments such as the African Refugee Convention (1969) or the Cartagena Declaration on Refugees (1984).

➤ Clarify the meaning of terms that may be in use locally to refer to displaced persons and relate these local terms to the internationally recognized definitions of IDPs and refugees.

➤ For any mention of "durable solutions," specify exactly what that means in the specific context of internal displacement (i.e., return, local integration where IDPs were displaced to, settlement in another part of the country).

Incorporate Displacement-Specific Rights and Protections

When incorporating displacement-specific human rights and protections under international humanitarian law in a peace agreement, mediators should focus on addressing current internal displacement and work to incorporate provisions aimed at preventing future displacement (table 5). Preventive as well as protective lenses are required for truly durable solutions.

As stated earlier in this guide, IDPs are no less entitled than anyone else in their country to enjoy all human rights. However, certain rights are of particular relevance for IDPs given their unique needs and vulnerabilities, such as the right to choose return to their homes, local integration, or settlement elsewhere in the country, rights to restitution of property left behind, and rights to documentation.

Many peace agreements include guarantees of human rights for all the population—often specified in a "Bill of Rights" section—and for certain vulnerable groups, such as women and children. However, these guarantees often do not address displacement-specific needs and should be complemented by the incorporation of displacement-specific human rights.

Mediators should use the Guiding Principles, including the sections that group IDP rights and protections, as an organizing framework to ensure that the rights of IDPs are adequately integrated into the peace agreement.

Options and guidance for mediators

Use the mission statement presented in Step 2 as a framework for ensuring that the peace agreement is oriented toward finding durable solutions for displaced persons and communities who need to restart normal lives. In addition, work to ensure—taking into account the need to balance maximalist and pragmatic approaches, depending on the particular circumstances—that the peace agreement includes the following:

➤ *Reference to relevant norms:* Ensure the inclusion of an explicit reference to the Guiding Principles and relevant international, regional, and national human rights instruments, as well as to the duty of parties to the agreement to respect, protect, and fulfill these rights of IDPs and returnees.

➤ *Prohibition of discrimination:* Ensure the inclusion of provisions that IDPs and returnees must not be discriminated against, particularly on account of their ethnic origin, religious belief, or political opinion, or because they have been displaced.

➤ *Right to choose among solutions:* Ensure explicit recognition of the rights of IDPs to freely choose among voluntary return to their homes, local integration in areas to where they have been displaced, or settlement in another part of the country. Include a commitment from the parties to provide IDPs with all necessary information to make an informed decision regarding any of these durable solutions, to consult with IDPs, and, to the extent possible, to let IDPs participate in the planning and management options chosen.

➤ *Preconditions for durable solutions:* Ensure that the agreement addresses conditions necessary to enable IDPs to resume normal lives on a sustainable basis, in particular:

  • *Right to safety and security:* Ensure, where relevant, the inclusion of provisions regarding humanitarian demining, demobilization, and disarmament of combatants and deployment of law enforcement institutions and personnel in areas where IDPs will reside.

  • *Property rights:* Include provisions to guarantee the restitution of IDPs' property and ownership or, where this is not possible, adequate compensation, as well as provisions for mechanisms to facilitate identification of rightful owners. Ensure that the property rights of IDPs are reflected in any provisions of the agreement relating to land use and allocation or land tenure systems. Include guarantees of nondiscrimination in access to or restitution of ownership of land and other property.

- *Right to adequate standard of living and access to livelihoods:* Ensure inclusion of economic, social, and cultural rights, in particular relating to provision of and nondiscriminatory access to essential food, water, and sanitation; basic shelter and housing; health and education; and access to the labor market and other sources of livelihoods in areas where IDPs will reside.

- *Reconciliation:* Include provisions on reconciliation between returnees and local communities, where relevant.

➤ *Right to documentation:* Include provisions for providing IDPs with all required documentation to resume normal lives fully and to participate in political affairs, including the restitution of lost or destroyed documentation.

➤ *Right to family unity:* Where families have been separated during displacement, include provisions on tracing missing persons and family reunifications.

➤ *Political rights:* Ensure that IDPs can participate in post-conflict elections and referenda even if they have not returned to their former places of residence. Ensure guarantees for participation of IDPs in public affairs, including in interim and final political arrangements and appointed transitional authorities.

➤ *Right to reparation for past injustices:* Ensure inclusion of reparation for arbitrary displacement into schemes designed to redress past displacement.

Table 5. Examples of Incorporation of Displacement-Specific Rights and Protections

Context	Draft/Final Peace Agreement	Provision	Comment
Great Lakes	Pact on Security, Stability and Development in the Great Lakes Region	"Member States undertake ... to adopt and implement the Guiding Principles on Internal Displacement ..."	Explicit reference and commitment to implementation of the Guiding Principles
Bosnia-Herzegovina	Annex VII to the Dayton Accords	"The Parties shall ensure that refugees and displaced persons are permitted to return in safety, without risk of harassment, intimidation, persecution, or discrimination, particularly on account of their ethnic origin, religious belief, or political opinion."	IDP-specific prohibition of discrimination
Nepal	Comprehensive Peace Accord	"Both sides shall respect and protect the citizens' right to free mobility and the freedom to choose within legal norms the location of one's residence and express the commitment to respect the right of the people displaced by the conflict and their families to return back to their homes or to settle in any other location of their choice."	Explicit recognition of the right of IDPs to choose freely between return to their homes, local integration in areas to where they were displaced, or settlement in another part of the country
Sudan	Darfur Peace Agreement	"[Darfur Rehabilitation and Resettlement Commission (DRRC], in collaboration with the relevant authorities, ... shall issue to displaced persons all documents necessary for the exercise of their legal rights, such as passports, personal identification documents, birth certificates, marriage certificates and all necessary documents of title. In particular, DRRC shall facilitate the issuance of new documents or the replacement of documents lost during displacement, without the imposition of unreasonable conditions, costs or delays."	Explicit obligation to provide relevant documentation to IDPs in a nondiscriminatory way
Kosovo	Interim Agreement for Peace and Self-Government in Kosovo	"The Commission shall adopt electoral Rules and Regulations on all matters necessary for the conduct of free and fair elections in Kosovo, including rules relating to: the eligibility and registration of candidates, parties, and voters, including displaced persons and refugees..."	Explicit reference to including IDPs as eligible voters in elections, confirming their rights under Guiding Principle 22

Incorporate Interests of IDPs

The rights and protections of IDPs that should be included in a peace agreement are defined in the Guiding Principles, which in turn reflects the rights and protections provided for by international humanitarian and human rights law. These rights and protections as such cannot, therefore, be negotiated during the peace process or diluted in any peace agreement.

However, IDPs may have specific concerns, views, and perspectives as regards the actual implementation of these rights and measures envisaged in these contexts. Such interests may be legitimately rooted in the IDPs' specific needs in a given context and should therefore be addressed (table 7).

For example, Principle 29 of the Guiding Principles specifies that "competent authorities have the duty and responsibility to assist returned and/or resettled internally displaced persons to recover, to the extent possible, their property and possessions which they left behind or were dispossessed of upon their displacement. When recovery of such property and possessions is not possible, competent authorities shall provide or assist these persons in obtaining appropriate compensation or another form of just reparation." Many options may be considered for possible compensation and reparations, and the interests of IDPs will assist in identifying what type of compensation or reparation will help to bring the most durable solution. Another example is the type of durable solution preferred by most. If most prefer, say, local integration rather than return, the agreement should specifically address this solution and not just deal with measures relevant for return.

Options and guidance for mediators

➤ Work to reflect the interests of IDPs in the specific way that their rights are incorporated in the peace agreement.

➤ Where a number of options are available, use the interests of IDPs to assist in identifying the most appropriate solution.

Table 7. Example of Incorporation of the Interests of IDPs

Context	Draft/ Final Peace Agreement	Provision	Comment
Sierra Leone	Lomé Peace Agreement	"As a reaffirmation of their commitment to the obser-vation of the conventions and principles of human rights ..., the Parties shall take effective and appropri-ate measures to ensure ... that no camps or dwellings of refugees or displaced persons are violated."	Addresses the concerns of IDPs about a lack of security in camps and dwellings as a context-specific aspect of the right to security

Specify Roles and Obligations of Relevant Actors with Regard to IDPs

Peace agreements—separately from specifying the rights and protections afforded to IDPs—should identify the roles and obligations of the parties and other actors toward IDPs (table 8). Once again, the Guiding Principles can assist in specifying the duties and obligations of actors toward IDPs.

Options and guidance for mediators

➤ Include specification of the roles and obligations of the parties to the conflict—whether national authorities or nonstate armed groups—to prevent further displacement and to ensure the fulfillment of the rights and protections during displacement and during return or settlement. Some examples include the following:

- Refer to the text of Guiding Principle 28 for duties and obligations of competent authorities to establish conditions for voluntary return, local integration or settlement elsewhere in the country. (Paragraph 1 of Guiding Principle 28 states: "Competent authorities have the primary duty and responsibility to establish conditions, as well as provide the means, which allow internally displaced persons to return voluntarily, in safety and with dignity, to their homes or places of habitual residence, or to resettle voluntarily in another part of the

country. Such authorities shall endeavour to facilitate the
reintegration of returned or resettled internally displaced persons.")

- Refer to the text of Guiding Principle 30 for duties and obligations to
facilitate rapid and unimpeded humanitarian access. (Guiding
Principle 30 declares, "All authorities concerned shall grant and
facilitate for international humanitarian organizations and other
appropriate actors, in the exercise of their respective mandates, rapid
and unimpeded access to internally displaced persons to assist in
their return or resettlement and reintegration.")

➤ Include specification of the roles and obligations of other actors—
including international humanitarian organizations and, where relevant,
third-party states or intergovernmental regional bodies—to prevent
further displacement and to ensure fulfillment of the rights and
protections during displacement and during return, local integration, or
settlement elsewhere in the country.

➤ Identify mechanisms for monitoring compliance of the parties regarding
their commitments to IDPs.

➤ Identify consequences and measures to be taken in the event that parties
abrogate their responsibilities to IDPs.

Table 8. Examples of Specification of Roles and Obligations of Actors with Respect to IDPs

Context	Draft/Final Peace Agreement	Provisions	Comment
Nepal	Comprehensive Peace Agreement	"Both sides agree to form a National Peace and Rehabilitation Commission to establish peace in the society by normalizing adverse situations generated by armed conflict and to carry out relief for and rehabilitate people victimized and displaced by war, and to carry forward the tasks related to this through the Commission."	Designates the creation of a specific entity to provide relief and rehabilitation services for IDPs and returnees
Sudan	Darfur Peace Agreement	"DRRC shall, in accordance with its regulations, grant the United Nations, NGOs and other humanitarian agencies access to displaced and war-affected persons, whether they are in urban, rural or camp settings, in accordance with international humanitarian law. Disputes over humanitarian access shall be referred to the relevant national government authorities."	Clarifies that the DRRC (Darfur Rehabilitation and Resettlement Commission) will be responsible for ensuring compliance with Guiding Principle 30 and specifies who will handle disputes

Address Implementation

Two options exist for addressing implementation in peace agreements: implementation of the agreement can be specified within the text of the agreement itself, or implementation can be specified in protocols or documents separate from the main agreement. The former option can make implementation provisions more explicit and can tie the parties more directly into their respective implementation roles.

IDP Perspectives
Nepal: Ensuring a Comprehensive Approach to the Implementation of IDP Return

The Comprehensive Peace Agreement concluded between the Government of Nepal and the Communist Party of Nepal (Maoist) in November 2006 included provisions pertaining to the IDPs' right of return: "Both sides express commitment to allow without any political prejudice the people displaced during the armed conflict to return voluntarily to their respective places of ancestral or former residence, to reconstruct the infrastructure destroyed as a result of the conflict and to honourably rehabilitate and reintegrate the displaced people into the society."

However, implementation of these provisions continues to face many challenges. According to one IDP (displaced for eight years): "I asked the [government] Chief District Officer to arrange security for me to return, but he told me that he couldn't promise anything and rather asked me to stay in the capital for my safety . . . Now how can I return?"

The government has acknowledged the challenges: "Our district offices have been trying their best to provide support to the IDPs, but they themselves are overburdened with security tasks," admitted Durga Nidhi Sharma, the Ministry of Peace and Reconstruction's joint secretary.

He added that the government planned to provide IDPs with poverty alleviation programs, free education, health care, and employment. But he explained that the situation was exacerbated by insufficient data with which to create an accurate picture of the IDP situation.

IDPs stated they want more aid and not just transportation costs to return to their places of origin.

Source: United Nations Integrated Regional Information Network (IRIN), *NEPAL: IDPs Still Waiting for Help, Despite Peace Accord* (Kathmandu: IRIN, 6 August 2008).

When it comes to devising the specific provisions for implementation, mediators should consider a variety of substantive issues, including what aspects of implementation of an agreement relate specifically to IDPs, what it will cost to implement the IDP-specific provisions, how the IDP-specific provisions link with other provisions of an agreement (i.e., the "cross-linkages"), the time frame for implementation, the security considerations and provisions that most acutely relate to implementation of the IDP-specific provisions, and the sequence of implementation of IDP-specific provisions (table 9).

Options and guidance for mediators

➤ Define clearly the mandate and composition of any entity established to monitor implementation of the agreement. Identify the specific role(s) IDPs will play in this entity and any associated monitoring and evaluation activities.

➤ Identify quantitative and qualitative milestones to be achieved in implementing provisions of the agreement relating to IDPs. These milestones need not necessarily be tied to a time frame.

➤ Specify the conditions to be met in implementing provisions for the voluntary return or settlement of IDPs.[12]

➤ Ensure that IDP-related provisions governing implementation are adequately reflected in other sections of the agreement. For example, ensure that the provisions dealing with implementation of durable solutions for the return, local integration, or settlement elsewhere in the country of IDPs are complemented by provisions relating to security and the roles of the parties in other parts of the agreement.

➤ Ensure the consideration of funding requirements for the implementation of provisions relating to IDPs.

➤ Include provisions to provide for the resolution of disputes arising from the implementation of IDP-specific provisions of the agreement. For example, include dispute-resolution mechanisms for resolving property ownership disputes that may arise if IDPs choose to return to their home communities.

Table 9. Examples of Provisions Relating to Implementation

Context	Draft/Final Peace Agreement	Provisions	Comment
Côte d'Ivoire	Ouagadougou Peace Agreement	"[T]he parties, the signatories to this agreement, agree to set up, as soon as possible, a programme of aid to the return of war displaced persons. The programme aims at facilitating the social integration of persons and families that abandoned their homes or assets because of the war. The two (2) parties agree on providing the concerned Technical Ministry with the means of implementing the programme."	Specifies that a program will be created and which ministry will implement it
Liberia	Comprehensive Peace Agreement between the Government of Liberia, LURD, MODEL, and Political Parties	"Establishment of a mission of the special representative to the ECOWAS Executive Secretary in Liberia to coordinate the implementation and coordination of political, social, economic, and security assistance with the UN mission and set up a monitoring mechanism for the implementation of the peace agreement."	Clearly establishes mechanism for international support to implement provisions of the peace agreement

Appendices

Appendix 1

Examples of the Inclusion of Internal Displacement in Recent Peace Agreements

The following table provides examples of peace agreements signed between 2003 and 2008 in situations that exhibited significant displacement. The agreements display varying degrees of inclusion (strong, weak, none) of internal displacement.

Country/Situation and Peace Agreement	Number of IDPs at Signing (Estimated)	Comment
Strong mention of internal displacement in the peace agreement		
Nepal Comprehensive Peace Agreement of 2006	100,000	Covers sixteen of the Guiding Principles; however, the agreement contains several areas of vague language pertaining to internal displacement.
Democratic Republic of the Congo (DRC) Inter-Congolese Political Negotiations of 2003	2,329,000	Covers eight of the Guiding Principles and recognizes within the document over three million IDPs.
Sudan Comprehensive Peace Agreement of 2005	3,000,000 4,000,000	Covers eight of the Guiding Principles. Many human rights are recognized as universal, but the agreement does not emphasize IDP-specific human rights per se.
Notably weak mention of internal displacement in the peace agreement		
Central African Republic Syrte Agreement of 2007	197,000	Only one very limited mention of internal displacement: Article 3.3 calls for the creation of conditions for return, resettlement, or reinsertion of the displaced.

Côte d'Ivoire Ouagadougou Peace Agreement of 2007	709,048	IDPs are addressed only once, in article 6.5 in terms of their return: *"Aid to the return of war displaced persons."* The preamble and article 6 reference the free movement of goods and people.
DRC North and South Kivu Ceasefire Agreements of 2008	1,400,000	Only two references to IDPs. Article 3 calls for the creation of a commission to oversee returns, in coordination with the United Nations and humanitarian organizations. Article 4.4 calls for the creation of a demilitarized zone to ensure safe returns.
No mention of internal displacement in the agreement		
Colombia Santa Fe de Ralito Peace Agreement of 2003	2,800,000	No reference to internal displacement. All recent peace processes and agreements for Colombia focus on demobilization and reintegration of armed actors, not on IDPs.
Indonesia/Aceh Memorandum of Understanding between Government of Indonesia and Free Aceh Movement of 2005	100,000	No reference to IDPs.
Somalia Communiqué issued by the Ministerial Committee Final Communiqué on the second round of talks of 2006	400,000 1,000,000	Neither communiqué makes reference to IDPs.

Appendix 2

Summary of Guiding Principles on Internal Displacement

	Principle	Provisions/Protections
Section I: **General Principles**	1	Equality and nondiscrimination of IDPs
	2	Wide scope of application and impartial, neutral nature
	3	Primary obligation of national authorities; right to request and receive protection from authorities
	4	Prohibition of discrimination; special protection for women, children, disabled, and elderly
Section II: **Principles Relating to Protection from Displacement**	5	Obligations under international law to prevent displacement
	6	Prohibition of arbitrary displacement, including ethnic cleansing, armed conflict, development projects, natural disasters, and collective punishment; limit on duration of displacement
	7	Duty to consider feasible alternatives to displacement; duty to ensure conditions of safety, nutrition, health, hygiene, and nonseparation of families; decision by empowered authority; duty to provide full information to, obtain consent from, and consult with IDPs; duty to provide law enforcement; judicial review and remedy
	8	Prohibition of displacement that violates rights to life, dignity, liberty, or security
	9	Special protections for land-dependent groups
Section III: **Principles Relating to Protection during Displacement**	10	Right to life, including protection against genocide, murder, summary or arbitrary executions, and enforced disappearances
	11	Right to dignity and physical, mental, and moral integrity; duty to protect IDPs from rape, torture, cruel treatment, gender-based violence, slavery, and terrorism
	12	Right to liberty and security; prohibition of arbitrary arrest or detention; protection from confinement, discriminatory arrest, and hostage-taking

	Principle	Provisions/Protections
	13	Nonparticipation of children in conflict; protection against recruitment into armed forces
	14	Right to freedom of movement, in particular in and out of camps
	15	IDP rights to seek safety, to leave their country, to seek asylum; duty to protect against forcible return
	16	Right to know the fate/whereabouts of relatives; duty to inform next of kin; duty to collect, identify, and return remains; duty to protect and provide access to gravesites
	17	Right to respect for family life; right of family to remain together; duty to reunite families; right to remain together in camps
	18	Right to adequate standard of living; duty to provide food, potable water, shelter, clothing, medical services, and sanitation; duty to ensure participation of women in provision of these supplies
	19	Right to medical care for sick, wounded, and disabled; right to psychological and social services; attention to female health needs; attention to AIDS and other infectious diseases
	20	Right to legal personhood; duty to issue and replace documents; equal rights for men and women to receive documents
	21	Protection of property and possessions; protection against destruction, use, appropriation, and occupation
	22	Right to freedom of thought, conscience, religion, opinion, and expression; right to seek employment; right to associate freely; right to vote; right to communicate in own language
	23	Right to education; duty to provide primary education and training facilities in IDP camps; duty to ensure female participation
Section IV: Principles Relating to Humanitarian Assistance	24	Humanity, impartiality of humanitarian assistance; duty to protect humanitarian assistance from diversion
	25	Humanitarian assistance and primary duty of national authorities; consent and free passage to international humanitarian organizations; access to IDPs
	26	Protection of humanitarian personnel and supplies
	27	Duties of international humanitarian actors; codes of conduct

	Principle	Provisions/Protections
Section V: **Principles Relating to** **Return, Resettlement,** **and Reintegration**	28	Responsibility to establish conditions and means for voluntary return, local integration, or settlement elsewhere in the country; duty to ensure participation of IDPs in the process of finding such durable solutions
	29	Prohibition of discrimination of returning IDPs; duty to assist IDPs in recovery or compensation for lost property or possessions
	30	Duty to provide unimpeded access of humanitarian organizations to assist return, local integration, or settlement elsewhere in the country

Appendix 3

Useful Resources

This list identifies select resources that can provide additional information and guidance to mediators dealing with issues related to internal displacement. These resources complement the information included in this guide and may be relied upon to strengthen understanding of the relationship of peace and internal displacement.

Type	Source	Description of Resource
Peace agreement libraries and databases	United States Institute of Peace http://www.usip.org	Peace agreement database and digital conflict library, over four hundred conflict management books and publications, conflict analysis online course, negotiation simulations, training center
	Beyond Intractability http://www.beyond intractability.org	Guides, essays, and information on peace agreements, peace processes, mediation and negotiation, and many other conflict-related topics
	Conciliation Resources http://www.c-r.org	Peace agreements index, accord publications, educational materials, policy briefings, reports, and working papers
Peace agreement drafting tools and resources	United Nations Peacemaker http://peacemaker. unlb.org/index1.php	Peace agreement database and summaries, drafting resources, humanitarian negotiations manual, legal library, lessons, case briefs, operational guidance, and knowledge essays
	Public International Law Policy Group http://www.public internationallaw. org/	Peace agreement drafter's handbook, negotiation simulations, backgrounders, and other publications
	International Council on Human Rights Policy http://www.ichrp. org/	Peace Agreements: The Role of Human Rights in Negotiations publication; human rights resources
Guiding Principles on Internal Displacement	Representative of the UN Secretary-General on the Human Rights of IDPs http://www2.ohchr. org/english/issues/ idp/issues.htm	Guiding Principles in over forty languages, legal bases for principles, annual reports and country visit reports, resolutions

Type	Source	Description of Resource
	Brookings-Bern Project on Internal Displacement http://www.brookings.edu/projects/idp.aspx	Guiding Principles in over forty languages and "Annotations to the Guiding Principles"; various publications, including *Addressing Internal Displacement in Peace Processes, Peace Agreements and Peace-Building, Addressing Internal Displacement: A Framework for National Responsibility,* and *Protecting Internally Displaced Persons: A Manual for Law and Policymakers.*
Internal displacement: documents and statistics	Internal Displacement Monitoring Center http://www.internal-displacement.org/	Country updates; maps; IDP document database; training modules on protection of IDPs
	United Nations Office of the High Commissioner for Refugees http://www.unhcr.org	Displacement statistics, *Annual State of the World's Refugees* and *Global Report* publications, legal handbooks, guidelines, training materials
Conflict analyses and databases	International Crisis Group http://www.crisis-group.org	Crisis Watch ongoing conflict database, conflict histories database, links to conflict research resources, conflict reports, and maps
	Uppsala Conflict Data Program http://www.pcr.uu.se/research/UCDP/index.htm	Database of armed organized violence and peacemaking efforts, data on content and implementation of peace agreements
Mediation support	UN Department of Political Affairs – Mediation Support Unit http://www.un.org/Depts/dpa/peace.html	Mediation lessons learned and best practices, mediation training, advice for practitioners, Mediation Support Standby Team
	Centre for Humanitarian Dialogue http://www.hdcentre.org	Publications on mediation, reports of the Oslo Forum
	Swisspeace – Mediation Support Project http://www.swisspeace.ch	Publications on mediation, Peace Mediation Essentials series, database of organizations active in mediation, mediation training

Notes

1. For a detailed analysis of the various aspects of the definition of "refugee" and guidance on determination of refugee status, see UN High Commissioner for Refugees, *Handbook on Procedures and Criteria for Determining Refugee Status under the 1951 Convention and the 1967 Protocol Relating to the Status of Refugees* (Geneva: UNHCR, re-edited 1992).

2. A brief background on the evolution of the Guiding Principles is provided on the Web site of the Office of the UN High Commissioner for Human Rights, http://www2.ohchr. org/english/issues/idp/standards.htm. Additional information on the Guiding Principles is provided on the Web site of the Brookings-Bern Project on Internal Displacement, www.brookings.edu/projects/idp/gp_page.aspx

3. 2005 World Summit Outcome, UN Doc. A/RES/60/ 1, para. 132.

4. See Jean-Marie Henckaerts and Louise Doswald-Beck, eds., *Customary International Humanitarian Law*, vols. 1 and 2 (Cambridge: Cambridge University Press, 2005). See, in particular, Rules 129–33.

5. Walter Kälin, *Guiding Principles on Internal Displacement: Annotations*, rev. ed., Studies in Transnational Legal Policy, no. 38 (Washington, DC: Brookings-Bern Project on Internal Displacement and the American Society of International Law, 2008). The annotations are also available at http://www.brookings.edu/projects/idp/publications.aspx.

6. See, for example, Security Council Resolution 1808 (2008) concerning the situation in Georgia, paragraph 9 of which reads: "Reiterates and reaffirms as fundamentally important the right of return for all the refugees and internally displaced persons to Abkhazia, Georgia, reaffirms the importance of such people's return to their home and property and that individual property rights have not been affected by the fact that owners had to flee during the conflict and that the residency rights and the identity of those owners will be respected, and calls on both sides to implement the UNHCR's Strategic Directions for the return in the first instance to the Gali region." Other examples include Security Council Resolution 1868 (2009), paragraph 4f, concerning the situation in Afghanistan; Security Council Resolution 1865 (2009), paragraph 14, concerning the situation in Cote d'Ivoire; the Security Council Resolution 1564 (2004), paragraph 6, concerning the situation in Sudan; and Security Council Resolution 1244 (1999), paragraph 7, on the situation in Kosovo.

7. Committee of Ministers Rec (2006) 6, Paragraph 11.

8. A range of experiences in broader public participation in peace processes is captured in Catherine Barnes, ed., *Owning the Process: Public Participation in Peacemaking*, Accord Issue no. 13 (London: Conciliation Resources, 2002).

9. The provisions of UN Security Council Resolution 1325 (2000) pertaining to fulfilling a gender perspective when negotiating and implementing peace agreements are included in the Resource Kit.

10. The case of Burundi provides a useful example of the two key issues presented in this section: where to place provisions on internal displacement, and how to balance maximalist and pragmatic approaches. In signing the Arusha Peace and Reconciliation Agreement (2000), the parties agreed to "Definitive resolution of the issues relating to refugees, displaced persons, regrouped persons, dispersed persons and other sinistrés" (Protocol I, Chapter II, Article 7) in accordance with the provisions of a protocol (Protocol IV) to the agreement. Protocol IV provided for the establishment of a "National Commission for the Rehabilitation of Sinistrés (CNRS), which [has] the mandate of organizing and coordinating, together with international organizations and countries of asylum, the return of refugees and sinistrés, assisting in their resettlement and reintegration, and dealing with all the other issues" (Article 3). The protocol also provided for the establishment of a Sub-Commission (of the CNRS) on Land. Land use and the right to return home or settle elsewhere were clearly priority issues in the negotiations between the parties to the conflict in Burundi; historically, land use and ownership had strongly influenced the dynamics of conflict in the country. See Prisca Mbura et al., "Land Access and the Return and Resettlement of IDPs and Refugees in Burundi" in Chris Huggins and Jenny Clover, eds., *From the Ground Up: Land Rights, Conflict and Peace in Sub-Saharan Africa* (Pretoria: Institute for Security Studies, 2005).

11. Several such studies are included in the Resource Kit that accompanies this guide. See, for example, Brookings-Bern Project on Internal Displacement, *Addressing Internal Displacement in Peace Processes, Peace Agreements and Peace-Building* (Washington, DC: Brookings Institution, 2007); Public International Law Policy Group, *Peace Agreement Drafter's Handbook* (Washington, DC: Public International Law Policy Group, 2005), especially the chapter on refugee return; International Council on Human Rights Policy, *Negotiating Justice? Human Rights and Peace Agreements* (Geneva: International Council on Human Rights Policy, 2006).

12. A listing of these conditions is provided in Brookings-Bern Project on Internal Displacement, *When Displacement Ends: A Framework for Durable Solutions* (Washington, DC: Brookings Institution, 2007), 14–17.

.

About the Lead Author

Gerard Mc Hugh is founder and president of Conflict Dynamics International, an independent, not-for-profit organization that works to prevent conflict and to alleviate humanitarian suffering resulting from conflict and other crises around the world. He has worked on several peace processes, mediation initiatives, and negotiations, most recently to support mediation efforts led by the United Nations and African Union under the Darfur Political Process. Part of his work to support the UN-AU Mediation Team focused on developing and coordinating implementation of a strategy to engage key civil society constituencies—including displaced persons—in the peace process. Between 2005 and 2007, he successfully completed three mandates as coordinator of the UN Security Council Panel of Experts concerning the Sudan.

Mc Hugh has authored and coauthored numerous articles, reports, and resources for peace and humanitarian practitioners on a range of topics, including Sanctions Assessment Handbook (Inter-Agency Standing Committee, 2004); Humanitarian Negotiations with Armed Groups: A Manual for Practitioners (United Nations, 2006); Strengthening Protection of Children through Accountability (Conflict Dynamics, 2009); and National Elections and Political Accommodation in the Sudan (Conflict Dynamics, 2009). The Brookings-Bern Project on Internal Displacement commissioned Conflict Dynamics to produce this guide.

About the Brookings-Bern Project on Internal Displacement

Since 1994, the Brookings Institution's Project on Internal Displacement has sought to promote the human rights of internally displaced persons through advocacy and research. In a unique partnership, the Project works with the representative of the UN secretary-general for the human rights of internally displaced persons to support the development and implementation of policies by governments, international organizations, and civil society that uphold the rights of IDPs. The Project prepares major studies and develops resources to strengthen the normative framework for IDP protections based on the Guiding Principles on Internal Displacement and works to enhance both the will and the capacity to protect IDPs.

For more information, contact:
Brookings-Bern Project on Internal Displacement
1775 Massachusetts Avenue, NW
Washington, DC 20036
Phone: +1 (202) 797-6168
Fax: +1 (202) 797-6003
E-mail: brookings-bern@brookings.edu
Web site: www.brookings.edu/idp

About the United States Institute of Peace

The United States Institute of Peace is an independent, nonpartisan institution established and funded by Congress. The Institute provides analysis, training, and tools to help prevent, manage, and end violent international conflicts, promote stability, and professionalize the field of peacebuilding.

Chairman of the Board: J. Robinson West

Vice Chairman: George E. Moose

President: Richard H. Solomon

Executive Vice President: Tara Sonenshine

Chief Financial Officer: Michael Graham

Board of Directors

J. Robinson West (Chairman), Chairman, PFC Energy, Washington, D.C.

George E. Moose (Vice Chairman), Adjunct Professor of Practice, The George Washington University, Washington, D.C.

Anne H. Cahn, Former Scholar in Residence, American University, Washington, D.C.

Chester A. Crocker, James R. Schlesinger Professor of Strategic Studies, School of Foreign Service, Georgetown University, Washington, D.C.

Ikram U. Khan, President, Quality Care Consultants, LLC, Las Vegas, Nev.

Kerry Kennedy, Human Rights Activist

Stephen D. Krasner, Graham H. Stuart Professor of International Relations at Stanford University

Jeremy A. Rabkin, Professor of Law, George Mason University, Arlington, Va.

Judy Van Rest, Executive Vice President, International Republican Institute, Washington, D.C.

Nancy Zirkin, Executive Vice President, Leadership Conference on Civil Rights

Members Ex Officio

Michael H. Posner, Assistant Secretary of State for Democracy, Human Rights, and Labor

James N. Miller, Principal Deputy Under Secretary of Defense for Policy

Ann E. Rondeau, Vice Admiral, U.S. Navy; President, National Defense University

Richard H. Solomon, President, United States Institute of Peace (nonvoting)